What's Your Angle? and 9 More Math Games

Super-Engaging, Easy Games That Reinforce Fractions, Decimals, Geometry, Algebra, and More

by Laura Meiselman

NEW YORK • TORONTO • LONDON • AUCKLAND • SYDNEY •
MEXICO CITY • NEW DELHI • HONG KONG • BUENOS AIRES

SCHOLASTIC
Teaching
Resources

Cover design by Anna Christian
Interior design by Susan Kass
Illustrations by Mike Moran

ISBN 0-439-43762-8
Copyright © 2003 by Laura Meiselman
All rights reserved.
Printed in the U.S.A.

2 3 4 5 6 7 8 9 10   40   09 08 07 06 05 04 03

Table of Contents

Whenever I tell people I'm a math teacher, they inevitably respond, "I'm not good at math," or worse, "I don't like math." But I love math! And I've found that it's not hard to get kids excited about math, too.

The key, of course, is to make it fun. *What's Your Angle? and 9 More Math Games* offers a variety of super-fun and engaging games that reinforce concepts in number operations, problem solving, geometry, algebra, and more.

Playing games is a great way for students to work together. Students stay focused longer when they are actively involved. When students are having a good time, they probably won't even realize they're "doing" math. Shh! Don't tell!

How to Use These Games

There are many ways you can integrate these games into your math program. Use them to reinforce a topic you have just taught or to review skills learned long ago. For example, say your students have just learned the four quadrants of the coordinate plane and have had some experience plotting points. Instead of asking them to plot more points, which will undoubtedly result in moans and groans, offer them a game. Pass out "You Deleted My Line Segment!" (p. 54) and your students will be practicing skills and enjoying themselves at the same time. Imagine that! Or, maybe you've noticed that your students are having some difficulties with fractions. Play "Math Jeopardy" (p. 10) and watch how competition fuels your students' accuracy.

You may want to consider designating Friday as "Game Day." It's a relaxing way to end the week, and students will surely look forward to it. (You might use this as a behavior incentive by having students "earn" the privilege of playing a game on Fridays.)

Playing games on the days leading to a vacation is also a good idea. Students often get so excited before holidays that they have difficulty focusing. Rather than fight to get their attention, review the order of operations with "I've Got Your Number" (p. 7) or practice percents with "Shopping Spree" (p. 31).

To increase your supply of games, challenge students to design their own. Give them a list of topics to choose from and watch how creative they can be. I've found that this assignment often gives students who do not typically succeed in the classroom a chance to shine. I've seen kids design wonderful, artistic game boards that they are really proud of. If you can encourage students to be successful in your classroom in ways other than just achieving high test scores, you will see a greater level of motivation in the classroom.

uction

Storing the Games

A great place to store all your games is in a plastic box with a lid. Here are other tips for storing your games:

- For each game, label a file folder with the game title and keep copies of corresponding recording sheets, game cards, or game boards inside.
- Put cut-up game cards inside a labeled envelope before storing them in the file folder.
- Laminate the game boards or glue them inside manila folders to keep them sturdy.

- Store game pieces (such as coins or buttons), dice, and markers in resealable plastic bags and put them in the appropriate file folder.

Make sure your box is always fully stocked with all the necessary supplies. You never know when the time to play a game will present itself.

Math can be a lot of fun. Students who play games in math class often feel successful "doing" math. We teachers can make a difference in how children feel about math. Let's get them to like it!

Resources

Burns, Marilyn. **A Collection of Math Lessons from Grades 3 Through 6.** Marilyn Burns Education Association, 1986.

Burns, Marilyn, and Cathy Humphreys. **A Collection of Math Lessons From Grades 6 Through 8.** Pearson Learning, 1990.

Cohen, Elizabeth G. **Designing Groupwork: Strategies for the Heterogeneous Classroom.** Teachers College Press, 1994.

Countryman, Joan. **Writing to Learn Mathematics, Strategies That Work, K–12.** Heinemann, 1992.

Krulik, Stephen, and Robert E. Reys (editors). **Problem Solving in School Mathematics, National Council of Teachers of Mathematics, 1980 Yearbook.** National Council of Teachers of Mathematics, 1980.

Correlations with the NCTM Standards

1. Number and Operations
2. Algebra
3. Geometry
4. Measurement
5. Data Analysis and Probability
6. Problem Solving
7. Reasoning and Proof
8. Communication
9. Connections
10. Representation

Title	Page	NCTM Standards
I've Got Your Number	7	1, 6, 7, 8, 10
Math Jeopardy	10	1, 2
Shopping Spree	31	1, 6, 7, 8, 9
X Marks the Spot	36	2, 6, 7, 9, 10
What's Your Angle?	44	1, 3, 4, 8, 10
Polygon Play	48	3, 8
You Deleted My Line Segment!	54	1, 3, 7, 8
1, 2, 3, Jump	56	1, 4
Hop to It	58	1, 5, 9, 10
What's Your Problem?	61	1, 2, 6, 7, 8, 9, 10

I've Got Your Number

Order of Operations

Objective:
Students work with the order of operations in a meaningful and fun way.

Players:
Whole class divided into pairs, or a small group of four players

Materials:
- Number Toss Recording Sheet (page 9)
- 5 dice
- Timer or watch with second hand

Why Play the Game?

Students often learn the order of operations (parentheses, exponents, multiplication, division, addition, and subtraction) by memorizing the mnemonic PEMDAS and reciting the chant "Please Excuse My Dear Aunt Sally." However, repeating this mnemonic doesn't guarantee that students can compute numeric or algebraic phrases correctly. In this game, students practice manipulating numbers so they internalize the order of operations and develop a clearer number sense.

As students become more familiar with playing the game with others, you may want to give them time to work independently. Each student writes down the numbers that the teacher tosses and solves the problems on his or her own.

For a more challenging version of this game, use a deck of cards, assigning aces as 1's, Jacks as 11's, Queens as 12's, and Kings as 13's. You may want to allow calculators for this activity.

Getting Ready

Challenge students to write a number sentence using four 4's and the correct order of operations to equal the number 0. (For example, $4 - 4 + 4 - 4 = 0$.) There is more than one solution, so encourage students to come up with different answers. Repeat this exercise using 4's to equal the numbers 1 to 9.

Photocopy and distribute the recording sheet to each pair or small group. Each group should assign a Recorder to record their answers on their sheet. If you're playing as a whole class, you may want to make an overhead transparency of the recording sheet.

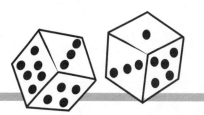

To Play:

1. Toss four dice and write each number on the recording sheet under the "Numbers" columns. Then toss the fifth die and record its number in the "Result" column. The goal is to write an equation using the first four numbers and the correct order of operations to result in the fifth number.

For example, say the first four numbers are 3, 3, 5, and 1, and the answer is 6. Using 3, 3, 5, and 1 and the four operations, exponents, or parentheses, how can you get 6? One answer is $(5 \times 3) \div 3 + 1$.

Note: In some instances, you'll find that no matter what operations you use, the first four numbers will not equal the fifth number. For example, if each of the first four numbers is 1 and the fifth number is 5, there is no solution. In such cases, just toss all five dice again.

2. Give students a specific time period in which to find a solution.

3. When time is up, invite each group to share their equation. You may want to ask one group to record their solution on the board or overhead transparency. Award each group a point for each correct solution.

4. Repeat steps 1 to 3.

Possible equations using four 4's to equal the numbers 1 to 9:

$$4 \div 4 + (4 - 4) = 1$$
$$4 - (4 + 4) \div 4 = 2$$
$$(4 + 4 + 4) \div 4 = 3$$
$$(4 - 4) \div 4 + 4 = 4$$
$$(4 + 4 \times 4) \div 4 = 5$$
$$4 + (4 + 4) \div 4 = 6$$
$$4 + 4 - 4 \div 4 = 7$$
$$4 + (4 \times 4) \div 4 = 8$$
$$4 + 4 + 4 \div 4 = 9$$

I've Got Your Number

Recording Sheet

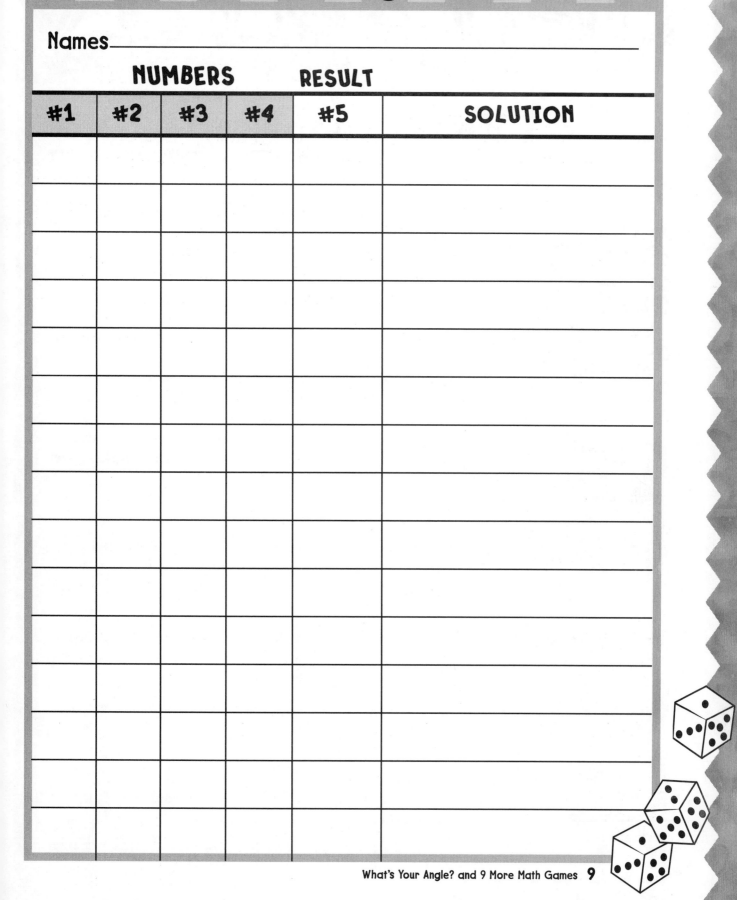

Names_____

NUMBERS				RESULT	
#1	#2	#3	#4	#5	SOLUTION

Math Jeopardy

Objective:

Students review fractions, decimals, percentages, and conversions.

Players:

Whole class divided into two teams, or a small group of four players

Materials:

- Math Jeopardy cards (pages 11–30)
- Clock or watch with a second hand
- Paper and pencil

Why Play the Game?

"Math Jeopardy" is a wonderful way to review the concepts of fractions, decimals, and percents that won't feel repetitive to students. It will also give you a sense of the particular skills that may need more attention. For example, if students find rewriting fractions as decimals a challenge, you may want to review that skill in your next lesson.

Getting Ready

Make double-sided copies of the Math Jeopardy cards. There are four categories: Fabulous Fractions, Darling Decimals, Perfect Percents, and Math Medley. Each category is divided into five different dollar values, and each dollar value contains eight cards.

Before playing, decide how much time players will have to answer a question. Choose a time limit that is suitable for students' age and level— one minute, 30 seconds, or 15 seconds.

If you're playing as a whole class, you may want to assign a Reader, Timer, and Scorekeeper. If students are playing in small groups, assign one player to keep track of everyone's totals.

To Play

1. Select four cards, each a different dollar value, from each category. (For a shorter version, select only two or three cards from each category.) Arrange the cards on the table according to category and dollar amount for easy access.

2. Each player starts with $500. Depending on the amount of money a player has, he chooses a category and a dollar amount. For example, he might say, "I'll have Darling Decimals for $200."

3. Read the card aloud. (In a small group, the person to the right of the player reads the card.) If the player answers correctly, he adds the card's dollar amount to his total. If not, he subtracts the money from his total. Put the card in a discard pile.

4. Play continues until all the cards have been discarded. The player with the most money at the end of the game wins.

Fabulous Fractions for $100

Fabulous Fractions for $100

Fabulous Fractions for $100

Fabulous Fractions for $100

Fabulous Fractions for $100

Fabulous Fractions for $100

Fabulous Fractions for $100

Fabulous Fractions for $100

Fabulous Fractions for $200

Fabulous Fractions for $200

Fabulous Fractions for $200

Fabulous Fractions for $200

Fabulous Fractions for $200

Fabulous Fractions for $200

Fabulous Fractions for $200

Fabulous Fractions for $200

Find the missing number in these equivalent fractions:

$$\frac{3}{5} = \frac{6}{x}$$

Answer: $x = 10$

Find the missing number in these equivalent fractions:

$$\frac{4}{8} = \frac{2}{x}$$

Answer: $x = 4$

Find the missing number in these equivalent fractions:

$$\frac{4}{6} = \frac{x}{12}$$

Answer: $x = 8$

Find the missing number in these equivalent fractions:

$$\frac{12}{36} = \frac{x}{72}$$

Answer: $x = 24$

Find the missing number in these equivalent fractions:

$$\frac{x}{12} = \frac{9}{36}$$

Answer: $x = 3$

Find the missing number in these equivalent fractions:

$$\frac{x}{25} = \frac{10}{50}$$

Answer: $x = 5$

Find the missing number in these equivalent fractions:

$$\frac{20}{30} = \frac{2}{x}$$

Answer: $x = 3$

Find the missing number in these equivalent fractions:

$$\frac{12}{18} = \frac{48}{x}$$

Answer: $x = 72$

Find the greatest common factor (GCF) of this pair of numbers:

(9, 3)

Answer: 3

Find the greatest common factor (GCF) of this pair of numbers:

(7, 10)

Answer: 1

Find the greatest common factor (GCF) of this pair of numbers:

(5, 10)

Answer: 5

Find the greatest common factor (GCF) of this pair of numbers:

(12, 8)

Answer: 4

Reduce this fraction to lowest terms:

$$\frac{4}{12}$$

Answer: $\frac{1}{3}$

Reduce this fraction to lowest terms:

$$\frac{10}{20}$$

Answer: $\frac{1}{2}$

Reduce this fraction to lowest terms:

$$\frac{18}{30}$$

Answer: $\frac{3}{5}$

Reduce this fraction to lowest terms:

$$\frac{14}{21}$$

Answer: $\frac{2}{3}$

Fabulous Fractions for $300	**Fabulous Fractions for $300**	**Fabulous Fractions for $300**	**Fabulous Fractions for $300**
Fabulous Fractions for $300	**Fabulous Fractions for $300**	**Fabulous Fractions for $300**	**Fabulous Fractions for $300**
Fabulous Fractions for $400	**Fabulous Fractions for $400**	**Fabulous Fractions for $400**	**Fabulous Fractions for $400**
Fabulous Fractions for $400	**Fabulous Fractions for $400**	**Fabulous Fractions for $400**	**Fabulous Fractions for $400**

Write this improper fraction as a mixed number in lowest terms:

$$\frac{9}{2}$$

Answer: $4\frac{1}{2}$

Write this improper fraction as a mixed number in lowest terms:

$$\frac{14}{3}$$

Answer: $4\frac{2}{3}$

Write this improper fraction as a mixed number in lowest terms:

$$\frac{8}{5}$$

Answer: $1\frac{3}{5}$

Write this improper fraction as a mixed number in lowest terms:

$$\frac{12}{5}$$

Answer: $2\frac{2}{5}$

Write this mixed number as an improper fraction in lowest terms:

$$3\frac{5}{9}$$

Answer: $\frac{32}{9}$

Write this mixed number as an improper fraction in lowest terms:

$$6\frac{3}{4}$$

Answer: $\frac{27}{4}$

Write this mixed number as an improper fraction in lowest terms:

$$16\frac{1}{2}$$

Answer: $\frac{33}{2}$

Write this mixed number as an improper fraction in lowest terms:

$$5\frac{4}{5}$$

Answer: $\frac{29}{5}$

Use <, >, or = to show the relationship between these fractions:

$$\frac{1}{5}, \frac{1}{4}$$

Answer: <

Use <, >, or = to show the relationship between these fractions:

$$\frac{5}{6}, \frac{3}{4}$$

Answer: >

Use <, >, or = to show the relationship between these fractions:

$$\frac{4}{5}, \frac{5}{8}$$

Answer: >

Use <, >, or = to show the relationship between these fractions:

$$\frac{7}{8}, \frac{28}{32}$$

Answer: =

Use <, >, or = to show the relationship between these fractions:

$$\frac{8}{12}, \frac{2}{3}$$

Answer: =

Use <, >, or = to show the relationship between these fractions:

$$\frac{1}{3}, \frac{3}{8}$$

Answer: <

Use <, >, or = to show the relationship between these fractions:

$$\frac{3}{4}, \frac{2}{5}$$

Answer: >

Use <, >, or = to show the relationship between these fractions:

$$\frac{7}{12}, \frac{3}{4}$$

Answer: <

Fabulous Fractions for $500	**Fabulous Fractions for $500**	**Fabulous Fractions for $500**	**Fabulous Fractions for $500**
Fabulous Fractions for $500	**Fabulous Fractions for $500**	**Fabulous Fractions for $500**	**Fabulous Fractions for $500**
Darling Decimals for $100	**Darling Decimals for $100**	**Darling Decimals for $100**	**Darling Decimals for $100**
Darling Decimals for $100	**Darling Decimals for $100**	**Darling Decimals for $100**	**Darling Decimals for $100**

Add and write the answer in lowest terms: $2\frac{1}{4} + 3\frac{2}{3}$ Answer: $5\frac{11}{12}$	**Add and write the answer in lowest terms:** $5\frac{3}{4} + 9\frac{5}{8}$ Answer: $15\frac{3}{8}$	**Add and write the answer in lowest terms:** $2\frac{2}{3} + 5\frac{1}{8}$ Answer: $7\frac{19}{24}$	**Subtract and write the answer in lowest terms:** $7\frac{1}{2} - 2\frac{1}{8}$ Answer: $5\frac{3}{8}$
Subtract and write the answer in lowest terms: $6\frac{2}{5} - 2\frac{1}{4}$ Answer: $4\frac{3}{20}$	**Subtract and write the answer in lowest terms:** $5\frac{1}{5} - 2\frac{3}{4}$ Answer: $2\frac{9}{20}$	**Subtract and write the answer in lowest terms:** $10\frac{1}{2} - 2\frac{5}{6}$ Answer: $7\frac{2}{3}$	**Add and write the answer in lowest terms:** $4\frac{2}{5} + 2\frac{5}{6}$ Answer: $7\frac{7}{30}$
Read this decimal aloud with correct place value: **0.003** Answer: three thousandths	**Read this decimal aloud with correct place value:** **0.045** Answer: forty-five thousandths	**Read this decimal aloud with correct place value:** **0.0005** Answer: five ten-thousandths	**Read this decimal aloud with correct place value:** **0.02** Answer: two hundredths
Read this decimal aloud with correct place value: **0.23** Answer: twenty-three hundredths	**Read this decimal aloud with correct place value:** **0.236** Answer: two hundred thirty-six thousandths	**Read this decimal aloud with correct place value:** **0.0033** Answer: thirty-three ten thousandths	**Read this decimal aloud with correct place value:** **2.3** Answer: two and three tenths

Darling Decimals for **$200**	**Darling** Decimals for **$200**	**Darling** Decimals for **$200**	**Darling** Decimals for **$200**
Darling Decimals for **$200**	**Darling** Decimals for **$200**	**Darling** Decimals for **$200**	**Darling** Decimals for **$200**
Darling Decimals for **$300**	**Darling** Decimals for **$300**	**Darling** Decimals for **$300**	**Darling** Decimals for **$300**
Darling Decimals for **$300**	**Darling** Decimals for **$300**	**Darling** Decimals for **$300**	**Darling** Decimals for **$300**

Use <, >, or = to show the relationship between these decimals:

0.2, 0.02

Answer: >

Use <, >, or = to show the relationship between these decimals:

0.43, 0.34

Answer: >

Use <, >, or = to show the relationship between these decimals:

0.622, 0.63

Answer: <

Use <, >, or = to show the relationship between these decimals:

4.05, 4.50

Answer: <

Use <, >, or = to show the relationship between these decimals:

0.003, 0.030

Answer: <

Use <, >, or = to show the relationship between these decimals:

0.07, 0.070

Answer: =

Use <, >, or = to show the relationship between these decimals:

0.56, 0.60

Answer: <

Use <, >, or = to show the relationship between these decimals:

15.9, 1.59

Answer: >

Round this decimal number to the nearest tenth:

0.78

Answer: 0.8

Round this decimal number to the nearest hundredth:

25.525

Answer: 25.53

Round this decimal number to the nearest whole number:

34.8

Answer: 35

Round this decimal number to the nearest tenth:

0.44

Answer: 0.4

Round this decimal number to the nearest hundredth:

200.319

Answer: 200.32

Round this decimal number to the nearest whole number:

2.3

Answer: 2

Round this decimal number to the nearest tenth:

0.93

Answer: 0.9

Round this decimal number to the nearest hundredth:

7.826

Answer: 7.83

Darling Decimals for $400	Darling Decimals for $400	Darling Decimals for $400	Darling Decimals for $400
Darling Decimals for $400	Darling Decimals for $400	Darling Decimals for $400	Darling Decimals for $400
Darling Decimals for $500	Darling Decimals for $500	Darling Decimals for $500	Darling Decimals for $500
Darling Decimals for $500	Darling Decimals for $500	Darling Decimals for $500	Darling Decimals for $500

Add the following decimal numbers: **29.2 + 18.8** **Answer:** 48	Subtract the following decimal numbers: **25.4 – 5.8** **Answer:** 19.6	Add the following decimal numbers: **1.33 + 22.6** **Answer:** 23.93	Subtract the following decimal numbers: **18.3 – 4.7** **Answer:** 13.6
Add the following decimal numbers: **79.04 + 7.8** **Answer:** 86.84	Subtract the following decimal numbers: **25.6 – 3.9** **Answer:** 21.7	Add the following decimal numbers: **0.45 + 0.85** **Answer:** 1.3	Subtract the following decimal numbers: **4.68 – 0.5** **Answer:** 4.18
Find the product: **3.2 x 0.3** **Answer:** 0.96	Find the product: **1.2 x 0.6** **Answer:** 0.72	Find the product: **5.5 x 0.03** **Answer:** 0.165	Find the product: **12 x 0.06** **Answer:** 0.72
Find the product: **0.4 x 0.02** **Answer:** 0.008	Find the product: **24 x 0.7** **Answer:** 16.8	Find the quotient: **95.7 ÷ 10** **Answer:** 9.57	Find the quotient: **233.4 ÷ 2** **Answer:** 116.7

Perfect Percents for **$100**	Perfect Percents for **$100**	Perfect Percents for **$100**	Perfect Percents for **$100**
Perfect Percents for **$100**	Perfect Percents for **$100**	Perfect Percents for **$100**	Perfect Percents for **$100**
Perfect Percents for **$200**	Perfect Percents for **$200**	Perfect Percents for **$200**	Perfect Percents for **$200**
Perfect Percents for **$200**	Perfect Percents for **$200**	Perfect Percents for **$200**	Perfect Percents for **$200**

12% of students in a class were late one day. What percent were on time?

Answer: 88%

35% of monkeys at the zoo are females. What percent are males?

Answer: 65%

30 of 100 boys play baseball. What percent is that?

Answer: 30%

A radio costs $100. The tax is 8%. How much money is the tax?

Answer: $8

74% of 100 cars are sports cars. How many cars are sports cars?

Answer: 74

29% of some beads are solid red and 17% are solid green. What percent are either red or green?

Answer: 46%

66% of the cookies are chocolate and 18% are sugar. What percent are either chocolate or sugar?

Answer: 84%

If you toss a penny, what percent of the time should it land heads up?

Answer: 50%

Write this decimal as a percent: **0.8**

Answer: 80%

Write this decimal as a percent: **0.5**

Answer: 50%

Write this decimal as a percent: **0.15**

Answer: 15%

Write this decimal as a percent: **1.65**

Answer: 165%

Find 20% of 300.

Answer: 60

Find 5% of 60.

Answer: 3

Find 25% of 400.

Answer: 100

Find 50% of 80.

Answer: 40

Perfect Percents for **$300**	**Perfect** Percents for **$300**	**Perfect** Percents for **$300**	**Perfect** Percents for **$300**
Perfect Percents for **$300**	**Perfect** Percents for **$300**	**Perfect** Percents for **$300**	**Perfect** Percents for **$300**
Perfect Percents for **$400**	**Perfect** Percents for **$400**	**Perfect** Percents for **$400**	**Perfect** Percents for **$400**
Perfect Percents for **$400**	**Perfect** Percents for **$400**	**Perfect** Percents for **$400**	**Perfect** Percents for **$400**

Write this fraction as a percent: $\dfrac{3}{20}$	Write this fraction as a percent: $\dfrac{7}{10}$	Write this fraction as a percent: $\dfrac{2}{5}$	Write this fraction as a percent: $\dfrac{1}{2}$
Answer: 15%	**Answer:** 70%	**Answer:** 40%	**Answer:** 50%
Write this fraction as a percent: $\dfrac{1}{4}$	Write this fraction as a percent: $\dfrac{3}{4}$	Write this fraction as a percent: $\dfrac{11}{20}$	Write this fraction as a percent: $\dfrac{16}{25}$
Answer: 25%	**Answer:** 75%	**Answer:** 55%	**Answer:** 64%
Write as a fraction in lowest terms: **40**%	Write as a fraction in lowest terms: **80**%	Write as a fraction in lowest terms: **25**%	Write as a fraction in lowest terms: **10**%
Answer: $\dfrac{2}{5}$	**Answer:** $\dfrac{4}{5}$	**Answer:** $\dfrac{1}{4}$	**Answer:** $\dfrac{1}{10}$
Write as a fraction in lowest terms: **92**%	Write as a fraction in lowest terms: **4**%	Write as a fraction in lowest terms: **125**%	Write as a fraction in lowest terms: **101**%
Answer: $\dfrac{23}{25}$	**Answer:** $\dfrac{1}{25}$	**Answer:** $1\dfrac{1}{4}$	**Answer:** $1\dfrac{1}{100}$

Perfect Percents for $500

Perfect Percents for $500

Perfect Percents for $500

Perfect Percents for $500

Perfect Percents for $500

Perfect Percents for $500

Perfect Percents for $500

Perfect Percents for $500

Math Medley for $100

Math Medley for $100

Math Medley for $100

Math Medley for $100

Math Medley for $100

Math Medley for $100

Math Medley for $100

Math Medley for $100

Find the percent: **37% of 140**	Find the percent: **15% of 80**	Find the percent: **43% of 76**	Find the percent: **16% of 800**
Answer: 51.8	Answer: 12	Answer: 32.68	Answer: 128
Find the percent: **60% of 150**	Find the percent: **75% of 400**	Find the percent: **2% of 40**	Find the percent: **5% of 375**
Answer: 90	Answer: 300	Answer: 0.8	Answer: 18.75
Write as a decimal: $\frac{1}{4}$	Write as a decimal: $\frac{1}{8}$	Write as a decimal: **63.5%**	Write as a decimal: $\frac{7}{10}$
Answer: 0.25	Answer: 0.125	Answer: 0.635	Answer: 0.7
Write as a decimal: $\frac{8}{200}$	Write as a decimal: **6.5%**	Write as a decimal: $\frac{24}{25}$	Write as a decimal: $\frac{1}{2}$
Answer: 0.04	Answer: 0.065	Answer: 0.96	Answer: 0.5

Math Medley for **$200**	Math Medley for **$200**	Math Medley for **$200**	Math Medley for **$200**
Math Medley for **$200**	Math Medley for **$200**	Math Medley for **$200**	Math Medley for **$200**
Math Medley for **$300**	Math Medley for **$300**	Math Medley for **$300**	Math Medley for **$300**
Math Medley for **$300**	Math Medley for **$300**	Math Medley for **$300**	Math Medley for **$300**

Find the least common multiple (LCM) of this pair of numbers: **4, 12**	Find the least common multiple (LCM) of this pair of numbers: **7, 11**	Find the least common multiple (LCM) of this pair of numbers: **5, 15**	Find the least common multiple (LCM) of this pair of numbers: **6, 8**
Answer: 12	**Answer: 77**	**Answer: 15**	**Answer: 24**
Find the least common multiple (LCM) of this pair of numbers: **9, 12**	Find the least common multiple (LCM) of this pair of numbers: **6, 9**	Find the least common multiple (LCM) of this pair of numbers: **8, 12**	Find the least common multiple (LCM) of this pair of numbers: **10, 6**
Answer: 36	**Answer: 18**	**Answer: 24**	**Answer: 30**
Find the quotient: **190.3 ÷ 2**	Find the quotient: **45.27 ÷ 9**	Write as a percent: **0.87**	Write as a percent: **0.03**
Answer: 95.15	**Answer: 5.03**	**Answer: 87%**	**Answer: 3%**
Write as a percent: **2.25**	Write this fraction as a percent: $\frac{14}{25}$	Write this fraction as a percent: $\frac{30}{200}$	Write this fraction as a percent: $\frac{50}{200}$
Answer: 225%	**Answer: 56%**	**Answer: 15%**	**Answer: 25%**

Math Medley for $400

Math Medley for $400

Math Medley for $400

Math Medley for $400

Math Medley for $400

Math Medley for $400

Math Medley for $400

Math Medley for $400

Math Medley for $500

Math Medley for $500

Math Medley for $500

Math Medley for $500

Math Medley for $500

Math Medley for $500

Math Medley for $500

Math Medley for $500

Write this fraction in lowest terms: $\frac{25}{500}$ Answer: $\frac{1}{20}$	**Write this fraction in lowest terms:** $\frac{18}{45}$ Answer: $\frac{2}{5}$	**Write as a fraction in lowest terms:** **86**% Answer: $\frac{43}{50}$	**Write as a fraction in lowest terms:** **12**% Answer: $\frac{3}{25}$
Write as a fraction in lowest terms: **205**% Answer: $2\frac{1}{20}$	Use <, >, or = to show the relationship between these fractions. $\frac{7}{8}$, $\frac{7}{10}$ Answer: >	Use <, >, or = to show the relationship between these fractions. $\frac{12}{24}$, $\frac{3}{6}$ Answer: =	Use <, >, or = to show the relationship between these fractions. $\frac{5}{8}$, $\frac{7}{9}$ Answer: <
Write this percent as a fraction in lowest terms and a decimal: **2**% Answer: $\frac{1}{50}$, 0.02	Write this percent as a fraction in lowest terms and a decimal: **49**% Answer: $\frac{49}{100}$, 0.49	Write this percent as a fraction in lowest terms and a decimal: **30**% Answer: $\frac{3}{10}$, 0.3	Write this percent as a fraction in lowest terms and a decimal: **2.5**% Answer: $\frac{1}{40}$, 0.025
Write this decimal as a percent and as a fraction in lowest terms: **0.55** Answer: 55%, $\frac{11}{20}$	Write this decimal as a percent and as a fraction in lowest terms: **0.06** Answer: 6%, $\frac{3}{50}$	Write this decimal as a percent and as a fraction in lowest terms: **0.66** Answer: 66%, $\frac{33}{50}$	Write this decimal as a percent and as a fraction in lowest terms: **0.01** Answer: 1%, $\frac{1}{100}$

$hopping $pree

Percents, Mental Math

Why Play the Game?

Finding the percent of a number is more than just a math skill. Knowing how much you'll pay for a $50 shirt at a 25% off sale, or how much tip you should leave at a restaurant are important life skills. Working with percents can be more efficient for students if they learn how to find certain "key" percent amounts in their heads. For example, finding 10% of a number is easy: Just divide by 10. If you teach students these shortcuts (or better yet, challenge students to figure them out among themselves) and give them time to practice, you will be pleased to see how quickly they become comfortable with percents.

"Shopping Spree" uses numbers that lend themselves to this do-it-in-your-head strategy so that students get practice working with mental math. Students can then use this skill to estimate percentages when they are working with not-so-friendly numbers.

Getting Ready

Share these shortcuts with students:

To find 10%: Divide by 10*

To find 50%: Divide by 2

To find 25%: Divide by 4 (or divide by 2 and then 2 again)

To find 1%: Divide by 100*

You can also finesse the above percentages to figure out any percent without pencil and paper (or calculator):

To find 20%: Find 10% and multiply by 2

To find 51%: Find 50% of the number and 1% of the number and add them

To find 75%: Find 50% of the number and 25% of the number and add them

To find 15%: Find 10% of the number and half of that (which is 5%) and then add them

*You can also move the decimal point one place to the left for dividing by 10, and two places to the left for dividing by 100.

Objective:
Students find the percent of a number using mental math

Players:
2

Materials:
- Tag Sale cards (pages 33–34)
- Shopping Spree game board (page 35)
- Die
- Buttons or coins (game markers)
- Paper and pencil

When students seem to understand how to apply these shortcuts, invite them to play the game.

To Play

1. Each player chooses a game marker and places it on START. Shuffle the Tag Sale cards and place them facedown next to the game board.

2. Players take turns tossing a die to figure out how many spaces to move. If a player lands on a Shopping Spree space, she must pick a Tag Sale card and figure out how much money she saves. Each player should keep track (in writing) of how much money he or she has saved.

3. The game is over when a player reaches FINISH. Players compare their savings. The player who saved the most money wins.

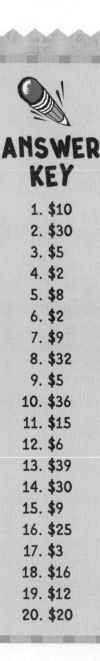

ANSWER KEY

1. $10
2. $30
3. $5
4. $2
5. $8
6. $2
7. $9
8. $32
9. $5
10. $36
11. $15
12. $6
13. $39
14. $30
15. $9
16. $25
17. $3
18. $16
19. $12
20. $20

Tag $ale Cards

1

Gadzooks! A sale
on polka-dotted underwear!
You save 20% on the $50 worth
you bought.

How much do you save?

2

CDs at 50% off...
too good to be true! You've got
to take advantage NOW! You buy
$60 worth of CDs.

How much do you save?

3

A special deal
on nose piercing ... will you be
able to talk your parents into it?
The regular price is $20, but
today it's 25% off.

**How much would you save if you
really went through with it?**

4

A large pizza
and a liter of soda
usually cost $20. You bring
a coupon from the local
newspaper and save 10%.

How much do you save?

5

Jumping
Jupiter!
$40 jeans at a 20% off sale.

**How many jelly beans (dollars)
do you save?**

6

Nightmare on Oak
Street, Part 27 is out,
and you've got to go! You have a
coupon that gives you 20% off
your ticket price of $10.

How much do you save?

7

Dad's birthday is
coming up and you see
the perfect tie. It's even more
perfect because it's on sale.

**How much will you save on a $30
tie that is 30% off?**

8

You strike it rich
at the local Papaya Republic.
Everything is 40% off. You gather
up $80 worth of clothes and bring
them to the register.

How much money will you save?

9

Okay, so 10% off
isn't much, but it's
something.

**How much do you save on a shirt
selling for $50?**

10

Annie's Antiques
wants to clear out some space in
the store. You see a mirror that you
know your mom will love. It's a steal
for 60% off $60.

How much would you save?

Tag $ale Cards

11

At the toy store,
you see a large pink sign announcing that all Berbie dolls and accessories are 25% off. You choose Belle of the Ball Berbie for your little cousin Mimi. Full price is $60.

How much do you save?

12

ShortNotes for the classics at 20% off.
You spot a few of Shakespeare's works that you need in school. They add up to $30 before the discount.

How much do you save?

13

Sneakers on sale!
Does it matter that you already have 10 pairs at home? The sneaks are regularly $130 and are on sale for 30% off.

How much do you save?

14

You never knew how cute
Rottweiler puppies could be. You realize you have enough money saved to buy the runt of the litter— a $200 puppy at 15% off.

How much do you save?

15

If you spend more than $50 at
Pappy's Pizzeria
they will give you 15% off. Sure enough, you and your hungry friends ate and drank $60 worth.

How much money do you save?

16

A new mountain bike
that usually sells for $500 is on sale for 5% off.

How much will you save on the bike?

17

Pink, purple, and green hairspray—
just what you need to update your look. You'll buy all three because, hey, they're on sale at 15% off.

How much do you save if the regular price for all three is $20?

18

Your cell phone fell in the toilet.
Yikes! You've got to get a new one quick —don't want to miss all those calls. The $80 Nokie is 20% off (and it's turquoise).

How much do you save?

19

Penny candy is
nowhere near a penny anymore. But if you buy 5 pounds of candy, you get 40% off. So you buy 5 pounds of gummy bears that normally cost $30.

How much do you save?

20

You buy ### school supplies
you don't really need right now because they're on sale for 25% off.

How much do you save on merchandise that totals $80?

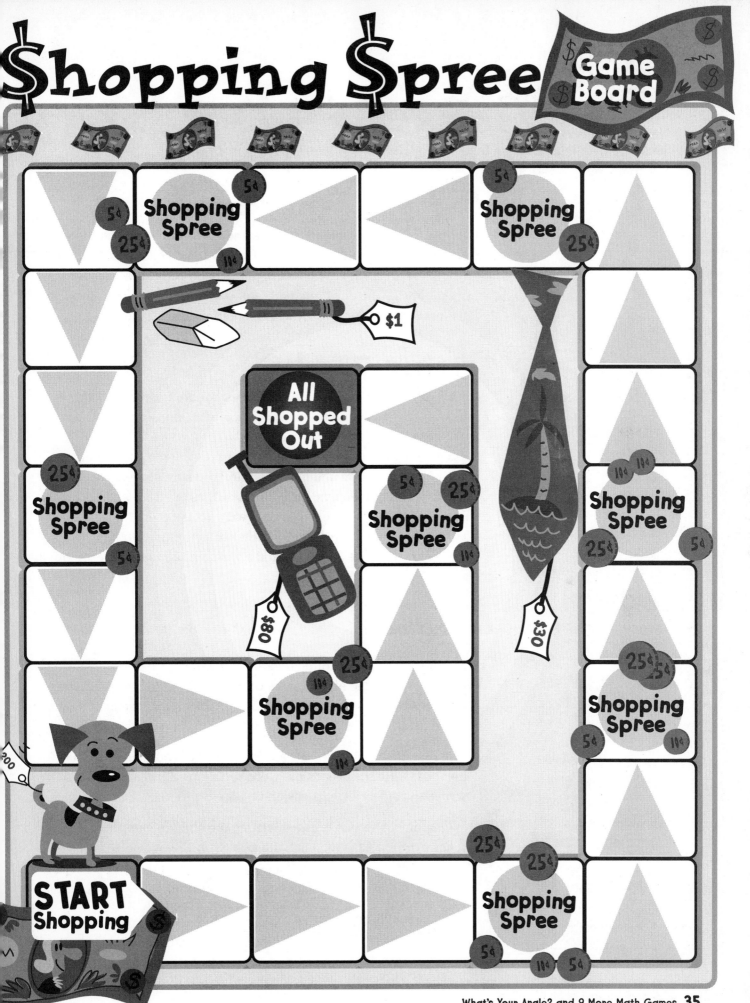

X Marks the Spot

Algebra

Why Play the Game?

Moving into the abstract realm of x's and y's can be a stretch for some kids. Before students can write and solve algebraic equations, they must first be comfortable with the concept of having a variable represent a quantity. "X Marks the Spot" includes some silly situations that give students practice working with variables and writing expressions.

Getting Ready

Make double-sided copies of the Express Yourself cards so that the correct answer appears on the back of each problem. Make several copies of the X's and O's and cut them apart.

Before playing the game, you may want to review the commutative property of both addition and multiplication. Be sure students know that $2 + t$ and $t + 2$ are equivalent expressions, as are $h \times 3$ and $3 \times h$. Depending on students' levels, you may want to ask them to use the raised dot to indicate multiplication rather than the traditional x, or show them how to write a number and a variable right next to each other, such as $3h$.

To Play

1. Shuffle the Express Yourself cards and place a card (problem side up) on each of the nine squares of the Tic-Tac-Toe board. Players choose whether they want to be X or O. Place the stacks of X and O cards next to the game board.

2. The first player chooses the space where he would like to place his X or O. He then reads the word problem on the card aloud and writes the algebraic expression on paper.

3. When the player has finished writing the algebraic expression, he turns over the card to check the answer. If the player is correct, he can place his X or O on that spot. If not, the other player gets to put her X or O there. The next player takes a turn.

4. The game continues with players taking turns until one gets three X's or O's in a row.

Objective:
Students practice writing algebraic expressions.

Players:
2

Materials:
- Express Yourself game cards (pages 37–42)
- Tic-Tac-Toe game board (page 43)
- X's and O's (page 43)
- Paper and pencil

Express Yourself Game Cards

Matilda Mudhead is m years old. Her sister Molly is half her age. Write an algebraic expression for Molly's age.

Franny has to wear her braces for t years. Carlos has to wear his braces for 2 years more than Franny does. Write an algebraic expression for the number of years Carlos has to wear braces.

Shamika received 5 A's on math tests this year. Her friend Natalie earned r fewer A's on her tests. Write an algebraic expression for the number of A's Natalie received.

Fernando caught x frogs in Patterson Pond. Jose caught 3 more than twice the number of frogs as Fernando. Write an algebraic expression for the number of frogs that Jose caught.

The first angle Anna measured was h degrees. The second angle she measured was 5 degrees less than the first angle. Write an algebraic expression for the number of degrees in the second angle.

An isosceles triangle's two equal sides are each y units long. The third side is 5 units long. Write an algebraic expression for the perimeter of the triangle.

A rectangle's shorter side is t units long. Its longer side is 5 more than double the length of the shorter side. Write an algebraic expression for the length of the longer side.

A rectangle's shorter side is y units long. Its longer side is 2 less than 3 times the length of the shorter side. Write an algebraic expression for the length of the longer side.

Jennifer earns $5 an hour babysitting. Stephanie earns m dollars an hour more than Jennifer does. Write an algebraic expression for the amount Stephanie earns per hour babysitting.

John ate y pieces of pizza. His friend Bubba ate 4 times as many slices. Write an algebraic expression for the number of pieces Bubba ate.

Ellyn received f flowers from a secret admirer. Later, she received 3 times as many flowers from a second admirer. Write an algebraic expression for the number of flowers that Ellyn received from the second admirer.

Alfredo played p practical jokes on April Fool's Day. He got caught for 7 fewer jokes than he played. Write an algebraic expression for the number of jokes Alfredo got caught for.

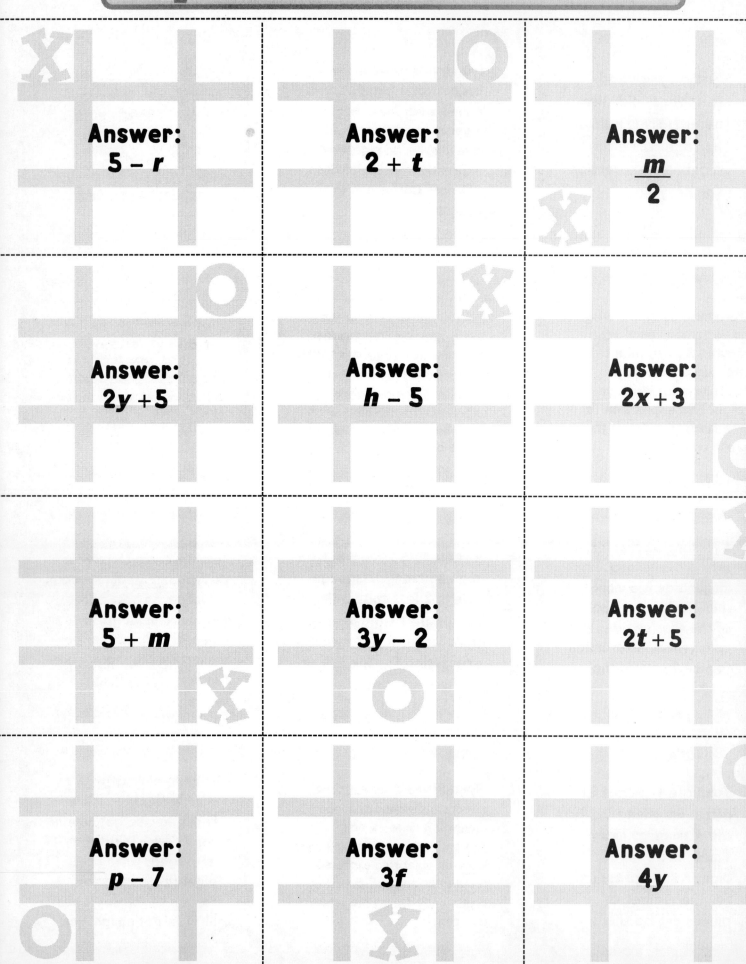

Answer:
5 – r

Answer:
2 + t

Answer:
$\dfrac{m}{2}$

Answer:
2y + 5

Answer:
h – 5

Answer:
2x + 3

Answer:
5 + m

Answer:
3y – 2

Answer:
2t + 5

Answer:
p – 7

Answer:
3f

Answer:
4y

Express Yourself Game Cards

Ryan bought *c* chocolate-frosted donuts. He bought 3 more honey-dipped donuts than chocolate-frosted donuts. Write an algebraic expression for the number of honey-dipped donuts Ryan bought.

Ling baked *x* chocolate chip cookies. She made 10 more than twice as many sugar cookies as chocolate chip cookies. Write an algebraic expression for the number of sugar cookies Ling baked.

Carla ran *m* miles last week. Paula ran 5 less than 3 times as many miles as Carla did. Write an algebraic expression to show the number of miles that Paula ran.

Louie collected *a* ants. Tyrone collected 5 fewer ants than Louie. Write an algebraic expression for the number of ants Tyrone collected.

Olivia stayed on the phone for 35 minutes. Alicia was on the phone *n* fewer minutes than Olivia, and Carlos was on the phone for 10 minutes longer than Alicia. Write an algebraic expression for the number of minutes that Carlos was on the phone.

Aaron bought a new pair of inline skates for *t* dollars. Estaban paid 1 more dollar than Aaron did. Write an algebraic expression for how much Estaban paid for the skates.

Vladimir made *v* baskets on Sunday afternoon. Juan made 1/4 as many baskets as Vladimir made. Write an algebraic expression for the number of baskets that Juan made.

Ursula is *p* inches tall. Nan is 6 inches shorter than Ursula. Tom is 1 inch taller than Nan. Write an algebraic expression for Tom's height in inches.

At a hotdog-eating contest, Zeke ate *z* hotdogs and expected to win. But Thor ate twice as many as Zeke did. Write an algebraic expression for the number of hotdogs that Thor ate.

Susie swam *s* miles at camp. Lizzie swam 5 more miles than Susie. Frizzie swam 1 mile less than Lizzie. Write an algebraic expression for the number of miles Frizzie swam.

Freddy watched 4 hours of TV on Saturday. Boris watched *b* more hours of TV than Freddy. Write an algebraic expression for the number of hours of TV that Boris watched.

Carla earned *d* dollars baby-sitting last weekend. Sarah earned 3 dollars less than twice as many dollars as Carla did. Write an algebraic expression for the number of dollars that Sarah earned.

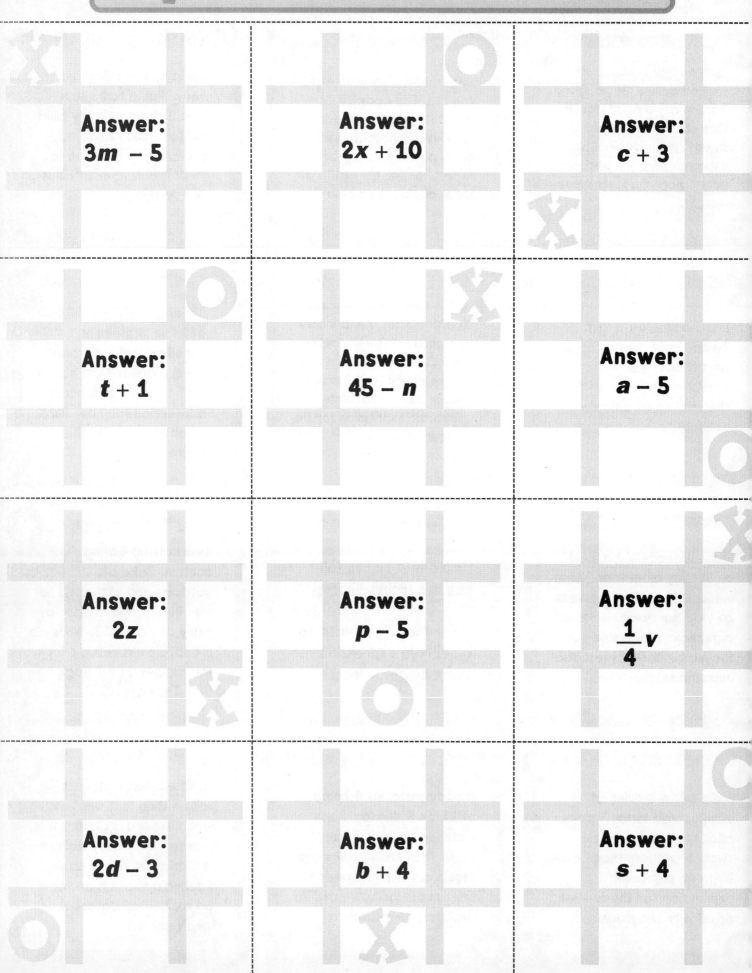

Answer:
$3m - 5$

Answer:
$2x + 10$

Answer:
$c + 3$

Answer:
$t + 1$

Answer:
$45 - n$

Answer:
$a - 5$

Answer:
$2z$

Answer:
$p - 5$

Answer:
$\frac{1}{4}v$

Answer:
$2d - 3$

Answer:
$b + 4$

Answer:
$s + 4$

Express Yourself Game Cards

Jojo claimed that there were g ghosts in his closet. Ming believed that she had 10 more ghosts in her closet than Jojo had in his. Write an algebraic expression for the number of ghosts in Ming's closet.

Ryan ate f pieces of peanut butter fudge. When his sister came home from school she ate 2 pieces less than Ryan ate. Write an algebraic expression for the number of pieces Ryan's sister ate.

Baby Benita soiled b diapers in the morning and one more than 3 times that many in the afternoon. Write an algebraic expression for the number of diapers that Baby Benita soiled in the afternoon.

On Friday Jared slam-dunked t times. Tino had a bad night and made 2 fewer slams than Jared. Write an algebraic expression for the number of slam dunks that Tino made.

Ike's new ice-cream parlor boasted f flavors. Mike's, across the street, carried 7 fewer flavors. Write an algebraic expression for the number of ice-cream flavors that Mike's carries.

Shirley had c curls bouncing all over her head. Yasmeen, however, had one more curl than Shirley. Write an algebraic expression for the number of curls both girls have together.

Hugo studied for m hours for his math test. Tyler studied 1 hour more than Hugo. Carlos studied twice as many hours as Tyler. Write an algebraic expression for the number of hours that Carlos studied.

Nicholas needed y dollars to buy a new skateboard. He had half as many dollars as he needed. Write an algebraic expression for the number of dollars that Nicholas has.

Shakia read s books. Natalie read 5 more than Shakia did. Hector read 1 less than Shakia did. Write an algebraic expression for the number of books that all three kids read.

Rhonda caught r fish at the lake. Her dad caught one more than half as many fish as she did. Write an algebraic expression for the number of fish that Rhonda's dad caught.

Booh had j jars of honey in his house. Bunny gave him 5 more jars. Write an algebraic expression for the number of jars Booh has now.

Jorge of the jungle swung from v vines last week. This week he swung from half as many. Write an algebraic expression for the number of vines that Jorge swung from this week.

Express Yourself Card Answers

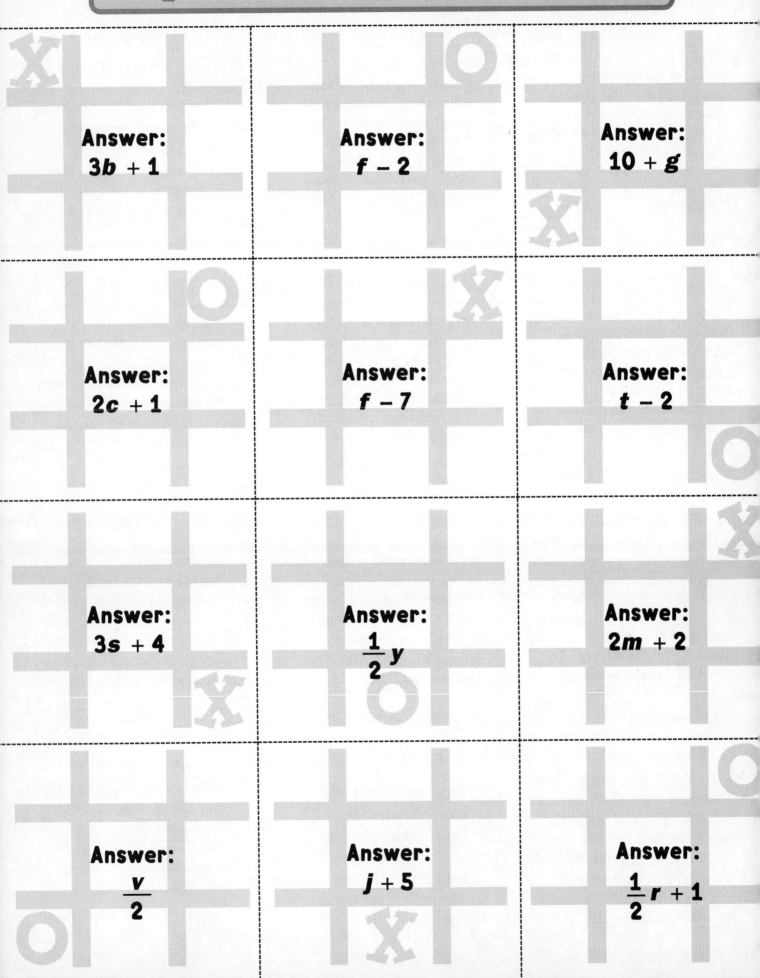

Answer:
$3b + 1$

Answer:
$f - 2$

Answer:
$10 + g$

Answer:
$2c + 1$

Answer:
$f - 7$

Answer:
$t - 2$

Answer:
$3s + 4$

Answer:
$\dfrac{1}{2}y$

Answer:
$2m + 2$

Answer:
$\dfrac{v}{2}$

Answer:
$j + 5$

Answer:
$\dfrac{1}{2}r + 1$

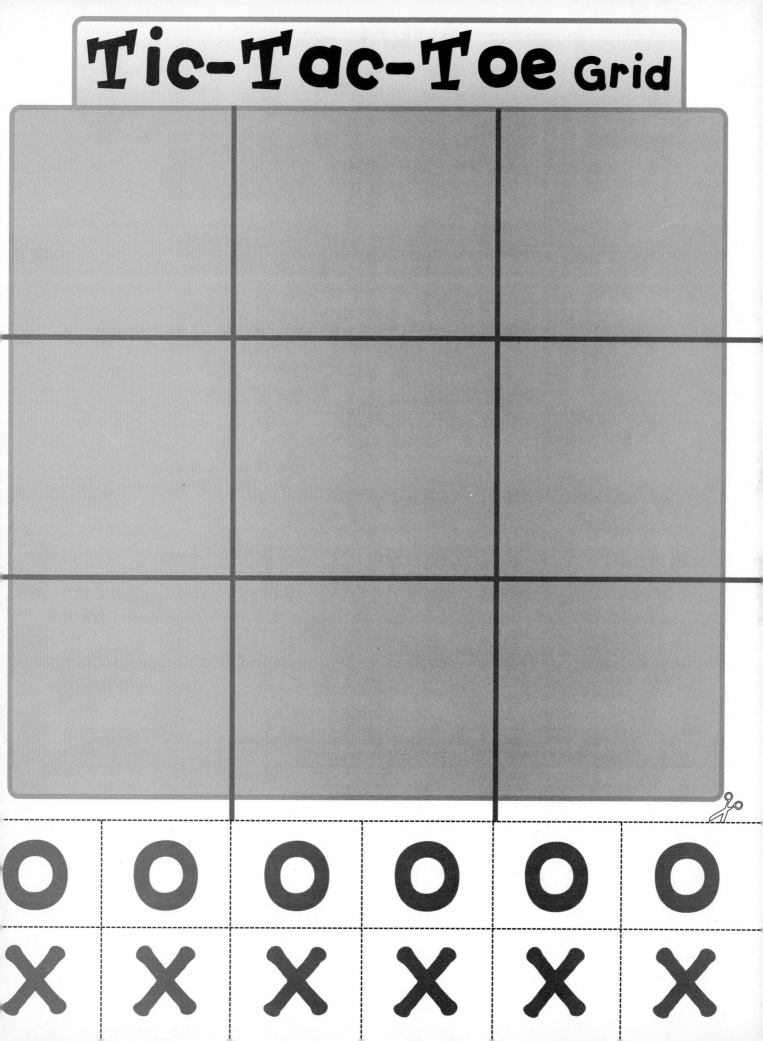

Tic-Tac-Toe Grid

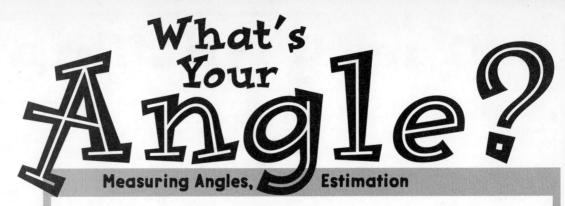

What's Your Angle?

Measuring Angles, Estimation

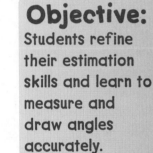

Objective:
Students refine their estimation skills and learn to measure and draw angles accurately.

Players:
2

Materials:
• Strange Angles sheet A or B (pages 45–46)
• What's Your Angle? Recording Sheet (page 47)
• Protractor

Why Play the Game?

Students can probably tell you that a 36-degree angle is acute, but they probably can't draw it—even with a protractor. In this game, students think they are competing against each other (which they love!), but they're actually competing against themselves. They refine their estimation skills and learn how to measure and draw angles more accurately. You can use students' completed recording sheets to assess their estimation skills.

Getting Ready

Photocopy one of the Strange Angles sheets and the recording sheet for each pair of players. (You can create additional angle sheets if students need more practice.)

To Play

1. Players look at the first angle in the What's Your Angle? sheet, and estimate how many degrees it has. Each player writes his or her guess on the recording sheet.

2. After estimating, players use the protractor to measure the angle. Have players take turns measuring with the protractor so that each student gets practice using it.

3. Have players use the following guidelines for scoring:

• If a player's estimate is exactly accurate, he earns 10 points.
• If a player's estimate is 1 or 2 degrees off, she earns 5 points.
• If a player's estimate is 3 to 9 degrees off, he earns 3 points.
• If a player's estimate is 10 or more degrees off, she doesn't earn any points.

4. After completing the sheet, players tally up their scores. The player with the highest score wins.

Strange Angles (Sheet A)

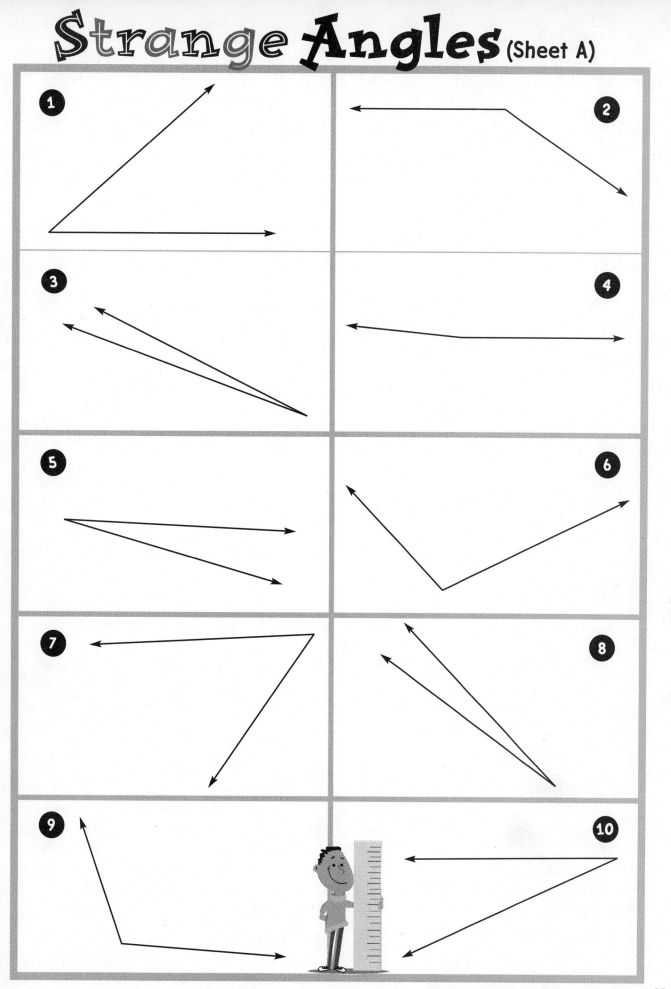

Strange Angles (Sheet B)

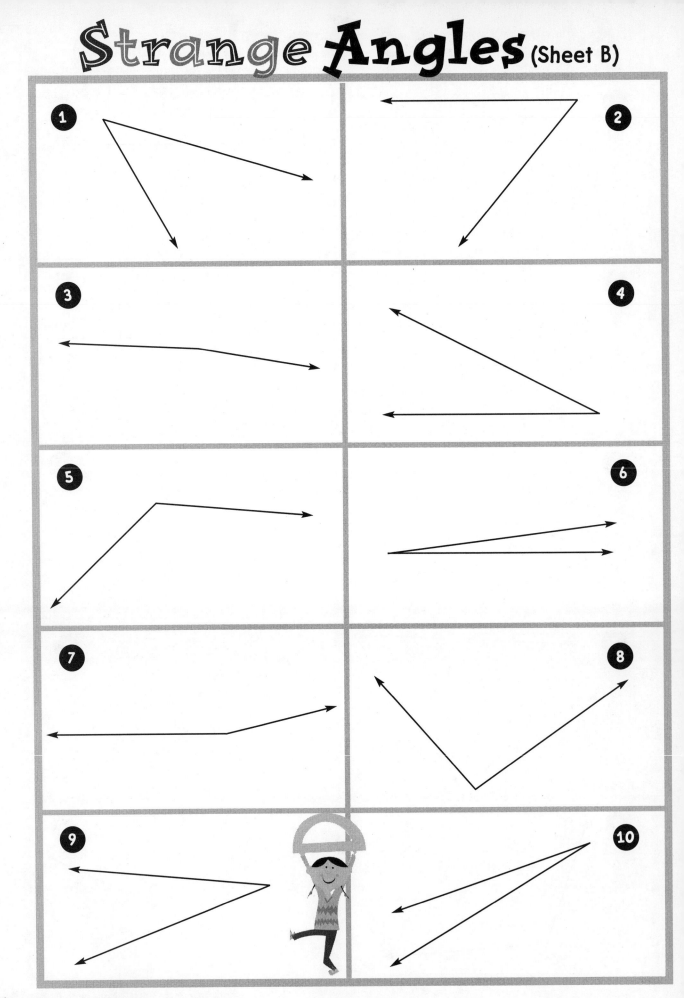

What's Your Angle? Recording Sheet

Player #1: _____   Player #2: _____

Record your estimates below. Calculate how many points you earn for each angle. Then add up the scores at the end of the game.

Scoring:

Exact measurement: 10 pts | 3 to 9 degrees off: 3 pts
1 or 2 degrees off: 5 pts | 10+ degrees off: 0 pts

	Player #1	Player #2	Actual Measure
Angle #1:	Estimate: _____ Points: _____	Estimate: _____ Points: _____	_____
Angle #2:	Estimate: _____ Points: _____	Estimate: _____ Points: _____	_____
Angle #3:	Estimate: _____ Points: _____	Estimate: _____ Points: _____	_____
Angle #4:	Estimate: _____ Points: _____	Estimate: _____ Points: _____	_____
Angle #5:	Estimate: _____ Points: _____	Estimate: _____ Points: _____	_____
Angle #6:	Estimate: _____ Points: _____	Estimate: _____ Points: _____	_____
Angle #7:	Estimate: _____ Points: _____	Estimate: _____ Points: _____	_____
Angle #8:	Estimate: _____ Points: _____	Estimate: _____ Points: _____	_____
Angle #9:	Estimate: _____ Points: _____	Estimate: _____ Points: _____	_____
Angle #10:	Estimate: _____ Points: _____	Estimate: _____ Points: _____	_____
	Total: _____	Total: _____	

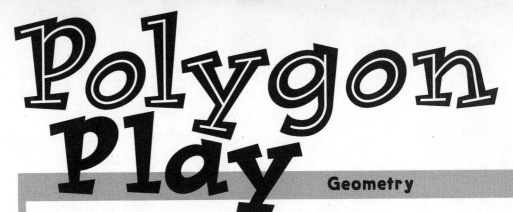

Polygon Play

Geometry

Objective:
Students become familiar with geometric vocabulary and follow directions to draw geometric figures.

Players:
2

Materials:
- Draw That Diagram! cards (pages 49–52)
- Polygon Play game board (page 53)
- Die
- Buttons or coins (game markers)
- Paper and pencil
- Protractor and ruler

Why Play the Game?

This game allows students to develop the ability to recognize and name a geometric shape, as well as draw geometric figures as described in the cards.

Getting Ready

Make double-sided copies of the Draw That Diagram! cards so that the correct diagram appears on the back of each instruction.

Review the following vocabulary with students: acute angle, acute triangle, circle, congruent, decagon, diagonal, diameter, equilateral triangle, hexagon, horizontal, hypotenuse, intersect, isosceles trapezoid, isosceles triangle, legs, line, line of symmetry, obtuse angle, obtuse triangle, octagon, opposite, parallel, parallelogram, pentagon, perimeter, perpendicular, point, radius, ray, rectangle, regular polygon, rhombus, right angle, right triangle, scalene triangle, segment, side, straight angle, square, trapezoid, and vertex.

To Play

1. Each player chooses a game marker and places it on START. Shuffle the Draw That Diagram! cards and place them instructions-side up next to the game board.

2. Players take turns tossing the die to figure out how many spaces to move.
- If a player lands on a space with a geometric figure, she must correctly name the figure to earn a point and move forward one space. If she cannot name the figure correctly, she stays in place and earns no points.

> **GAME BOARD ANSWER KEY** (clockwise from START):
>
> square, pentagon, equilateral triangle, rectangle, right triangle, rhombus, octagon, isosceles triangle, hexagon, decagon, trapezoid

- If a player lands on a DRAW space, he picks a card and draws the figure as described on the instructions. When finished, the player turns over the card to see the actual figure. If the pictures match, the player earns a point and moves forward one space. If they don't, the player stays in place and earns no points.

3. Play continues until one player earns 10 points. That player wins.

Draw a horizontal and a vertical line that intersect each other.

Draw a right triangle. Indicate the right angle with the appropriate mark. Label the hypotenuse 5 cm.

Draw a hexagon. Select one of the vertices of the hexagon and draw all diagonals possible.

Draw a straight angle horizontally. Above the line draw an isosceles triangle whose one shortest side lies on the straight angle.

Draw a scalene triangle. Draw a dotted line from one of the vertices so that it is perpendicular to the opposite side.

Draw a circle. Draw two radii that form an acute angle.

Draw horizontal segment $\overline{AB}$ and segment $\overline{CD}$ parallel to it of congruent length.

Draw a square. Draw its diagonals.

Draw an octagon. Draw an equilateral triangle that shares a side with the octagon. Have the triangle lie outside the octagon.

Draw a rectangle. Draw its lines of symmetry.

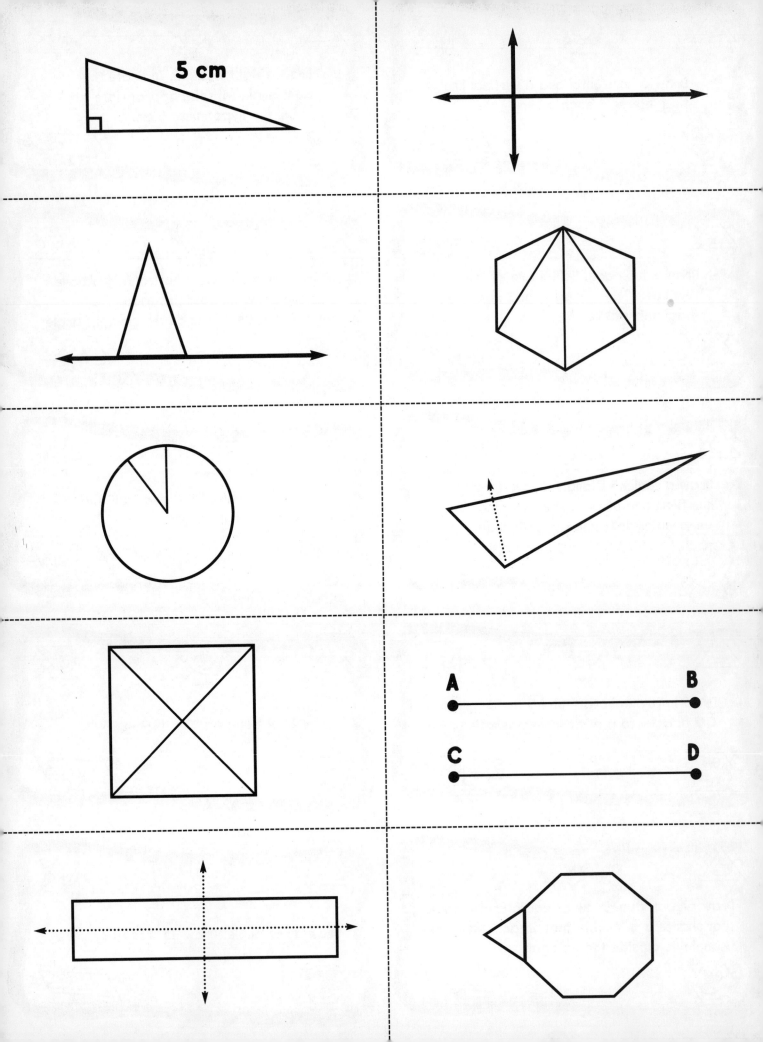

Draw a rhombus. Draw its shortest diagonal.

Draw a circle. Draw a diameter. Label the center of the circle **X**. Draw a ray from the center of the circle so that you have formed two right angles.

Draw an isosceles trapezoid. Inside the trapezoid draw a circle with center **P** and radius $\overline{PU}$.

Draw a right triangle and label the point with the right angle **Y**. Draw segment $\overline{YT}$ that makes a right angle outside of the triangle.

Draw a square. Use one of the sides as the side of an obtuse triangle lying outside the square. Using the opposite side of the square from the one where the obtuse triangle is, draw an equilateral triangle.

Draw a parallelogram with two acute and two obtuse angles. Draw two line segments inside the parallelogram so that they are parallel to the longer sides.

Draw an octagon. Label one of the vertices **V** and draw all the diagonals from that vertex. Draw ray $\overrightarrow{VR}$ so that it lies outside the octagon (except for point V, which is one of the octagon's vertices).

Draw two line segments that intersect at point **P**. Draw ray $\overrightarrow{PU}$ so that it lies between the two line segments.

Draw an obtuse angle. Draw a segment connecting a point on each of the rays so that you make a scalene triangle.

Draw an acute triangle. Using one of the sides, draw a rectangle so that it lies outside the acute triangle.

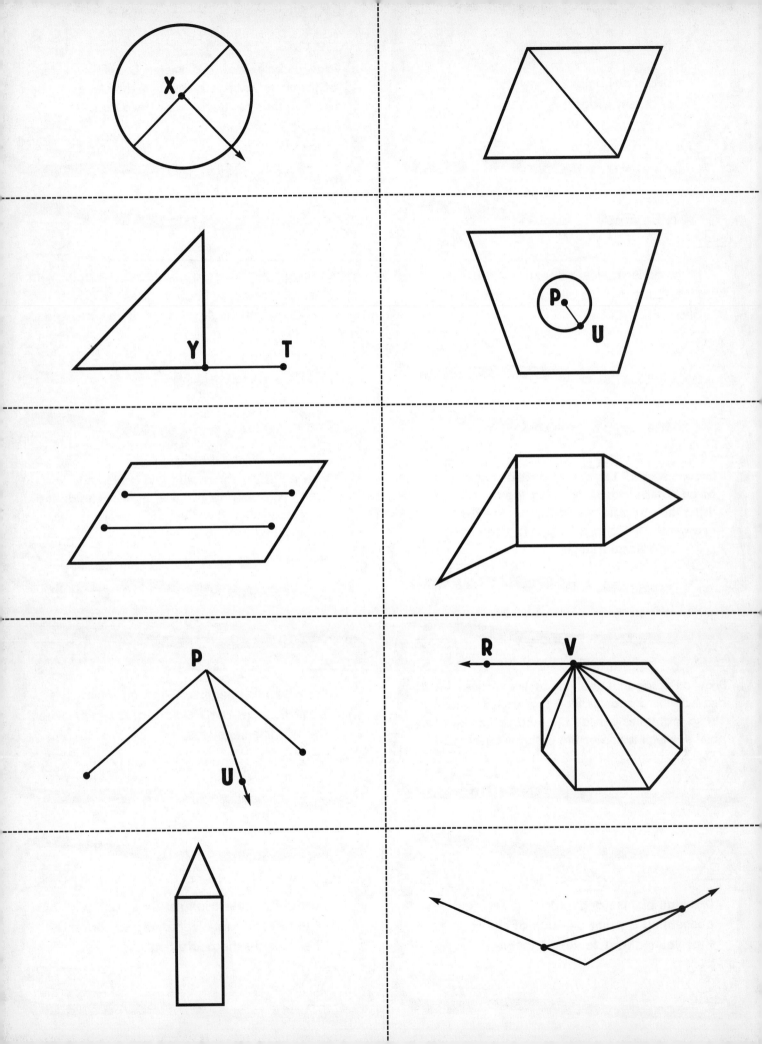

DRAW

START

DRAW

DRAW

DRAW

Polygon
Play
Game
Board

You Deleted My Line Segment!

(5, -4) (1, 2)

Coordinates

Why Play the Game?

This game is great for helping students feel more comfortable working on the coordinate plane. Players must locate particular points both to try to hit their opponent's point and to see whether one of their points has been hit. Students get many opportunities to practice finding points.

Getting Ready

Provide players with two copies of the Battle Lines Coordinate Grid—one to mark their line segments on, and another to record the hits and misses of their opponent's line segments. Players can use manila folders as screens to keep opponents from seeing their grids.

Objective:
Students practice plotting and locating points on the coordinate plane.

Players:
2

Materials:
(for each player)
- 2 Battle Lines Coordinate Grid (page 55)
- Red, black, and green pens
- Manila folder

To Play

1. Players use a black pen to draw their line segments on one coordinate grid. Each player draws five line segments on his grid: one 2 units long (3 dots long), two 4 units long (5 dots), and two 6 units long (7 dots). Segments may be horizontal, vertical, or diagonal, and may lie partially or completely on either axis.

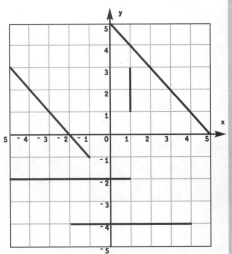

2. Players take turns trying to locate their opponent's segments by calling out a coordinate. For example, the first player may say, (+1, –4). The other player will say whether or not he has hit the point.

If a player gets a hit, he uses a green pen to mark the hit on his second coordinate grid. He may then call out another coordinate until he misses. If the player misses, he uses a red pen to mark the miss. The other player takes a turn.

3. When all of the points on a player's line segment get "hit," she must call out, "You deleted my line segment!" The first player to delete all of the other's line segments wins.

Battle Lines
Coordinate Grid

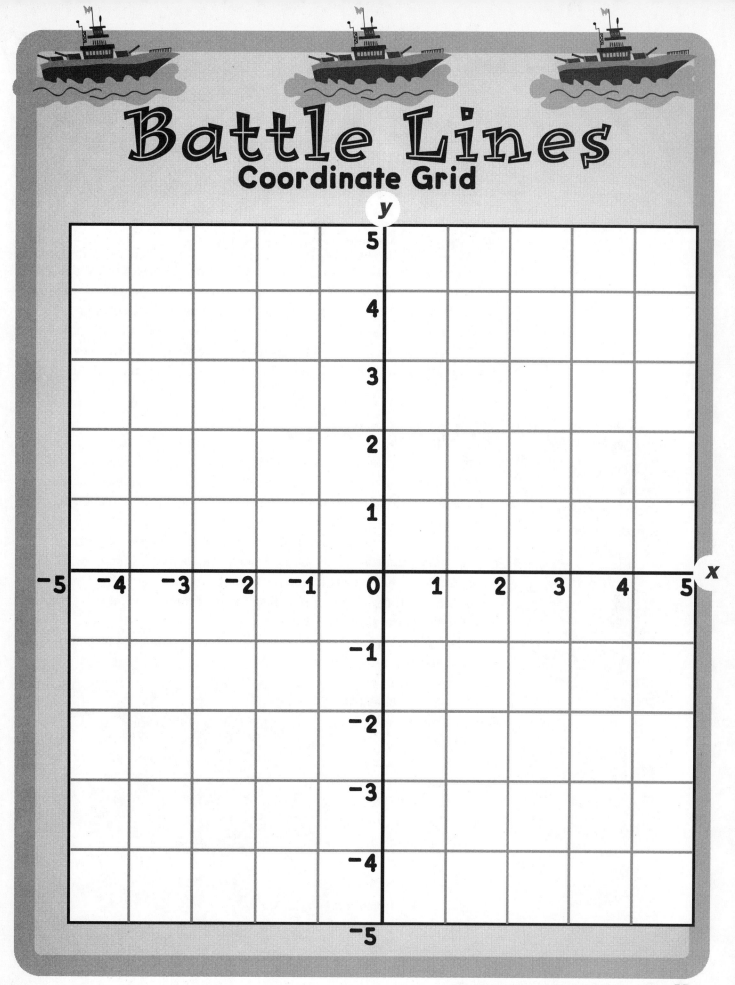

1,2,3 Jump!

Measurement, Metric System

Why Play the Game?

When students are given experiences that allow them to work with measurements, they begin to understand those measurements in a concrete rather than abstract way. This game offers students opportunities to take measurements while having fun. You may even want to extend the activity and have students practice conversions with the measurements they collect. For example, how many meters is 124 centimeters? How many millimeters?

Getting Ready

Divide the class into groups of four. Encourage students to name their group to give them a sense of unity (and a little fun!). Provide each group with a 2-foot strip of masking tape, a meter stick, and paper and pencil. Players in each group will have rotating roles of *jumper* (jumps), *marker* (marks where the jumper lands), *measurer* (measures the distance jumped), and *recorder* (records the distance jumped). The distance jumped will be measured from the starting line to the point farthest away; therefore, advise jumpers to fall forward rather than backwards. (You may want to let players do a couple of practice jumps for warm up.)

Enlist each group's help in setting up an area for jumping, preferably one free of desks or other objects. An empty hallway is ideal. If the weather is nice, you may choose to do this activity outside. Have students place a 2-foot strip of masking tape on the floor to mark the starting line.

Objective:
Students become familiar with metric measurements.

Players:
Whole class divided into small groups of four players

Materials:
(for each group)
- Meter stick
- 2-foot strip masking tape
- Paper and pencil

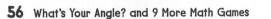

To Play

1. Players take turns doing the standing long jump. Jumpers should put their toes behind the strip of tape, bend their knees, swing their arms behind them, and propel themselves forward.

2. The measurer uses a meter stick to measure the distance between the starting line and the landing point. The recorder writes how many centimeters each player jumped. Round up measurements to the nearest centimeter.

3. After all players have jumped, each group should add up their measurements. The sum represents the total measurement for that group. Have each group record their measurement on the board or an overhead transparency for the other groups to copy.

4. Have students order the measurements from longest to shortest to identify the first-, second-, and third-place teams. (Optional: Reward the first-place team with small prizes, such as colorful pencils, stickers, or erasers.)

Extending the Activity

Now that students know how far they can jump, challenge them to jump an exact distance. Mark exactly 25 cm from the starting line and place a piece of tape there. Keeping students in their same groups as before, have each player try to jump exactly 25 cm. Assign someone to measure and record how many centimeters off the 25-cm mark each player jumped. Each group adds up the number of centimeters they (collectively) deviated from 25 cm. That number is their group's score. The group with the lowest score wins. Repeat this activity with 50 cm and 75 cm. Students will have a better sense of these measurements after completing the activity.

Hop to It

Objective:
Students collect data, then calculate and analyze measures of central tendency.

Players:
Whole class divided into small groups of four players

Materials:
- Hop to It Data Sheet (page 60)
- Timer or watch with a second hand
- Ping-Pong balls and paddles (for one activity)

Why Play the Game?

Math textbooks often provide sufficient practice for students to find the mean, median, mode, and range of a list of numbers. But they rarely help students understand how to collect or analyze real data. This game lets students "sink their teeth" into data analysis by giving them opportunities to collect their own data and work with them.

Students engage in different activities to collect data. If students do a different activity for each measure of central tendency, they may remember each method better by associating it with the activity that they were doing at the time. Of course, using one set of data to explore mean, median, mode, and range allows students to see what each number really signifies within one group of data.

Getting Ready

Photocopy the Hop to It data sheet for each student. Divide the class into small groups of four players each. Invite each group to choose from one of the following challenges:

- How many times can you hop on one foot with your hands on your head?

- How many times can you bounce a Ping-Pong ball on a paddle (straight up)?

- How many seconds does it take you to sing a verse of "Row, Row, Row Your Boat" (or some other nursery rhyme)?

- How many seconds can you keep your eyes open without blinking?

Assign each group a spot in the room to carry out an activity.

To Play

1. Players in each group take turns doing the chosen activity and counting or timing the activity. Each player records the data for every member of the group on his or her own data sheet.

2. After everyone has had a turn doing the activity, players work together to find the group's mean, median, mode, and range, and record them on the data sheets.

3. Invite a volunteer from each group to come up and record their group's data on an overhead transparency or the board. The group with the highest score in each measure of central tendency wins.

Extending the Activity

Invite students to write their personal data on the board or overhead transparency one at a time. Then challenge students to find the whole class's mean, median, mode, and range.

Hop to It Data Sheet

Name: _____

Activity: _____

Student	Data

Mean _____

Median _____

Mode _____

Range _____

What's Your Problem?

Problem Solving

Why Play the Game?

Problem solving is a skill that needs to be taught like any other. Students may not always know how to approach a problem, so we need to explicitly teach students some of the strategies they can use to solve problems. Among the most common strategies are:

A) Guess and check

B) Work backwards

C) Solve an easier problem

D) Draw a diagram or picture

E) Use a table or chart

F) Look for a pattern

G) Write and solve an algebraic equation

Each problem lends itself to some methods more than others.

Getting Ready

Photocopy and cut apart the Solve 'Em cards. Pick a problem and use it to introduce a particular problem-solving strategy to the class. Invite students to play "What's Your Problem?" instructing them to keep their eyes open for problems that can be solved using the same strategy you presented. Ask them to share those problems with the class after the game. Each time you play the game, highlight a different problem-solving strategy. This way, students become exposed to many different methods one at a time. (Next to the answers for each problem are the letters of relevant strategies. Use these letters as guides for presenting a problem that uses a particular method. Or, if students are stuck, you might want to suggest a method to get them on their way.)

Depending on the age and level of your students, decide how many problems each pair of players will solve at one time, and how much time they'll have to solve each problem. For younger students, one problem may be enough; for older ones, you may want to pass out three or four at a time.

continued

ANSWER KEY

1. 8 quarters (A, E, G)
2. 5 (A, B)
3. 7 (A, B)
4. 3 (A, B)
5. 7, 8 (A, E)
6. 9, 11 (A, E)
7. 3, 12 (A, E)
8. 98, 99 (A, E)
9. 101, 102 (A, E)
10. 12, 13, 14 (A, E)
11. 17, 18, 19 (A, E)
12. 25, 26, 27 (A, E)
13. $45 (A, B)
14. 8 years (A, D, G)
15. 38 weeks (A, D, G)
16. 8 months old (A, D, G)
17. 16 inches and 20 inches (A, D, E, G)
18. length = 10 in., width = 8 in. (A, D, E, G)
19. 80 degrees each (A, D)
20. 100 (A, C, G)
21. 6 photos (D)
22. 24 outfits (D)
23. $3\frac{3}{4}$ cups (C, G)
24. $26.32 (G)
25. $2.51 (B)
26. 8 miles: 7 @ .60 and 1 @ $2 (A, D, G)
27. 6 bounces (B, C, D)
28. 6 (D)
29. 4 coins; 3 quarters, 1 nickel (A, E)
30. 3 quarters, 2 dimes, 3 nickels, OR 2 quarters, 6 dimes (A, E)
31. length = 12 cm, width = 8 cm (A, D, E)
32. 60 inches (D)

You may also consider putting up a poster that identifies the steps in problem solving. The following is taken from George Polya's book, *Problem Solving in School Mathematics* (National Council of Teachers of Mathematics, 1980):

1. **Understand the problem** — Reading the problem is not enough—students must actually understand what the problem is asking. Encourage students to read the problem several times, underline key words, numbers, or pertinent information, then rephrase the problem to a classmate.

2. **Devise a plan** — To decide how to proceed, a student should ask himself questions like, "Should I draw a picture? Would a chart help? Have I seen a problem like this before?"

3. **Carry out the plan** — It's also a good idea to write down an estimate before doing the problem. For example, a student might write, "The taxi ride will cost about $10."

4. **Examine the solution obtained** — After figuring out the exact solution, a student should compare her answer with her estimate. If the answer seems reasonable, she should look again at the original problem to make sure she has answered the particular question asked.

As a final step, I ask my students to write a complete sentence with the information that they have found. For example, "The cab ride would cost Sophia $12.50." Writing the answer in a sentence brings students back to the details of the problem.

To Play

1. Divide the class into pairs. Give each pair a different set of problems to solve together.

2. When time is up, award each pair a point for each problem they have correctly solved.

3. Play as many rounds of the game as you like. The pairs with the top three scores are the winners.

Solve 'Em Cards

1. Antonio has only nickels and quarters. If he has 36 coins that total $3.40, how many of the coins are quarters?

2. I'm thinking of a number. If I multiply by 3 and then add 6, I get 21. What is the number?

3. I'm thinking of a number. If I multiply it by 5 and then add 9, I get 44. What is the number?

4. I'm thinking of a number. If I multiply it by 11 and subtract 8, I get 25. What is the number?

5. Find two numbers with a product of 56 and a sum of 15.

6. Find two numbers with a product of 99 and a sum of 20.

7. Find two numbers with a sum of 15 and a product of 36.

8. You open your math book and notice that the product of two consecutive page numbers is 9,702. What are the two page numbers?

9. The product of two consecutive page numbers in your science book is 10,302. What are the two page numbers?

10. The sum of three consecutive integers is 39. What are the three integers?

11. The sum of three consecutive integers is 54. What are the three integers?

12. The sum of three consecutive integers is 78. What are the three integers?

13. Sophia spent $5, then spent half of what she had left. Finally, she bought a soda for $1 and had $19 left. How much money did Sophia have at the beginning of the day?

14. A flower in the garden is $4\frac{1}{2}$ inches tall. If the flower grows at a rate of $1\frac{1}{2}$ inches each year, after how many years will the flower be $16\frac{1}{2}$ tall?

15. Bart puts $2 in his piggy bank each week. If he has $14 in it now, after how many weeks will he have $90?

16. Billy the baby was born weighing 7.4 pounds. He is gaining weight at the rate of 1.2 pounds a month. How old will Billy be when he weighs exactly 17 pounds?

Solve 'Em Cards

17

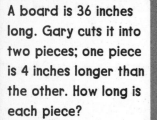

A board is 36 inches long. Gary cuts it into two pieces; one piece is 4 inches longer than the other. How long is each piece?

A rectangle has a perimeter of 36 inches. Its length is two inches greater than its width. How many inches is the width? the length?

18

19

In an isosceles triangle, there is only one angle that measures 20 degrees. What are the measures of each of the other two angles?

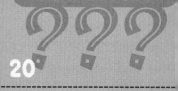

Sammy's mean average on three math tests was 92. He earned an 87 on his first test and an 89 on his second test. What score did he receive on his third test?

20

21

Mr. Jones wants to take a photo of his triplets, Hugh, Sue, and Drew, sitting in a row on the couch. If Mr. Jones wants to take every different order possible, how many different photos must he take?

Little Emma chooses a pair of tights, a dress, and a matching pair of shoes each morning. If she has 4 pairs of tights, 2 dresses, and 3 pairs of shoes, how many different outfits can Emma make?

22

23

Carla plans to bake 5 dozen cookies. The recipe she has is only for 2 dozen cookies and uses $1\frac{1}{2}$ cups of flour. How many cups of flour will Carla need to make 5 dozen cookies?

Tyrell ordered 3.5 pounds of ham, which costs $7.52 a pound. How much did he have to pay?

24

25

Jessie bought a CD for $9.99 and a poster for $7.50. How much change did he receive from his $20 bill?

Talaya's Taxi Service charges $2 for the first mile and $.60 for each additional mile. How many miles would you be able to travel for $6.20 (not including a tip)?

26

27

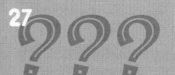

A ball is dropped from 80 feet. After each bounce, the ball's height is half of what it was with the previous bounce. After how many bounces will the ball be at 1.25 feet?

Manuel wanted three different flavors of ice cream on a cone, but he couldn't figure out in what order he should have them placed. Can you help him? How many different ways are there?

28

29

Greg had 80 cents in his pocket. He did not have any pennies or 50-cent pieces. What is the least number of coins Greg could have? Name them.

Hannah found some change on the sidewalk. How many of each coin did Hannah find if she found $1.10 and there were exactly 8 coins? (There were no dollar or 50-cent pieces.)

31

The length of a rectangle is 4 centimeters more than the width of the rectangle. If the area of the rectangle is 96 square centimeters, what would be the measures of the length and width?

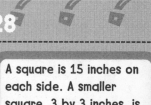

A square is 15 inches on each side. A smaller square, 3 by 3 inches, is cut from each corner of the larger square. What is the perimeter of the figure formed after the four smaller squares are cut out?

30

32